Loose
Ends
Bernadette Cremin

Loose Ends
© Bernadette Cremin and Pighog Press 2012

Bernadette Cremin has asserted her right to be identified as
the author of this work in accordance with the Copyright,
Designs and Patents Act 1998.

All rights reserved. No part of this pamphlet may be
reproduced, stored in a retrieval system, or transmitted in
any form, or by any means, electronic or otherwise, without
the prior written permission of Pighog Press.

This publication is sold subject to the condition that it shall
not, by way of trade or otherwise, be lent, resold, hired out
or otherwise circulated without the publisher's prior consent
in any form of binding or cover other than that in which it
is published and without a similar condition including this
condition being imposed on any subsequent purchaser.

A CIP record for this publication is available
from the British Library.

Design by curiouslondon.com

ISBN 978-1-906309-24-4
First published October 2012 by

Pighog Press
PO Box 145
Brighton BN1 6YU
England UK

info@pighog.co.uk
www.pighog.co.uk

Contents

The Morning After	5
Dead End	6
After Dark	8
False Start	9
Legacy	10
Cherry Pink	11
Happy Ending	12
Last Wish	13
Black	14
New Wound	16
Terminal	17
Mavis	18
Claudette	20
Still Life	22
Weird Fear	23
Italy	24
Dislocated	25
Drifter	26
Soft Inch	27
Unfinished Business	28
Surrender	30
Regret	31
Restless	32
Moving On	33

The Morning After

October's young light blanches the skyline,
a platinum sun leaks into the sea
between Brighton and West Pier.

A blur of cat's-eyes swerve the coast road
and milk floats bumble around suburbia
as bedsits fidget and hangovers hatch.

Letterboxes twitch like expectant fathers,
kettles flex, and mugs stand in dark cupboards
on draining boards in haphazard queues.

The city's plague of bus stops waits patiently
as a seduction of gulls hitches a thermal home.
I am blessed to witness such trust.

Nine cars throb at a red light fostering anger
at Brunswick Square, where the Peace Statue
provokes the lustful undertow of war.

A crow trespasses Pavilion Gardens
and gangs of windswept blossoms lurk
in gutters like pretty terrorists.

Dead End

Plugged into a suit for another week
of feigned interest, anonymous mistakes,
saving ten percent for my happy ending.

Another week of making ends meet, things fit,
in an office that smells of unfinished business.
I think of surfboards, the futility of regret but

I miss her too much on days like this.
I wonder where she lives, if she ever had kids?
My fat wife is fucking the butcher,

has been for all the years it's taken me
to pay off the mortgage, put my fat daughter
through college, afford a red car.

This morning I have a meeting
to discuss numbers, dates, targets
with voices. I think of surfboards.

My spray-tanned boss spills his weekend
across my ears, big tits, dumb heels, gin.
I yearn for the desire to be envious again.

I think of surfboards
imagine places I've never heard of,
languages I don't understand.

At lunchtime, I'll straighten my tie
for the pretty girl behind the counter
at Forfars and wish I was younger,

then, I'll buy the biggest cheapest box
of chocolates for my fat wife's birthday
a day late. She's fucking the butcher,

I can smell blood in her hair,
see her carving arguments
just to keep the noise down.

I can taste her raw tongue
on the drunken occasions
she rolls over to let me in.

When I fuck her
I think of the butcher,
the pretty girl at Forfars

and surfboards.

After Dark

Crows land on my eyelids,
stagger jagged tracks toward
my lipstick line and peck.

The mirror takes me hostage
as morning surveys the carnage,
my laughter has turned traitor.

Each smile leaves a tangled clue
to whom this mouth has tasted,
words its kissed and chewed.

Deep crevices, rat-tail thick
leave trails of days and nights,
crawling down my cheeks.

Age is an anxious art,
a creased map of flesh and skin –
the bubble that blunts the pin.

False Start

I waited, unwanted
like sour milk on her doorstep –

my feet on the E's of a filthy WELCOME mat
now bullied bald by years of boots and shoes.

Nine weeks she has had the keys
to this address she cannot read and so –

I am legally bound to save her from herself
while life pisses against my leg, a warm stink,

legally bound in spite of this migraine
and divorce that won't let me sleep.

I'm legally bound to tidy the mess she leaves
behind, lies that fester like sulking pain.

I'm legally bound to arrive with the police
between the postman and rent man

on the Crane Estate where Dr Penn
refuses to visit since the riot last May.

The judge had warned her to expect me today,
but I had warned the judge before the birth –

I knew that two small rooms and my weekly visit
would not contain her temper and premature son.

Legacy

Life has taught us not to bother
with each other's trivia,

but sometimes at bus stops,
in supermarket queues

or when weather becomes
suddenly significant

I miss you.

The smell of your pillow,
the heartless violet scar

tucked behind your ear
and wonder if you ever think

of that power cut, the spilt milk
the stain we never forgave.

Sometimes, I drink Sapphire gin
deliberately, to remind myself

why lemons and cinnamon exist
and look at those photographs,

tug my memory like a bully
but your legacy will always be

that drizzly Sunday in bed
listening to Sinatra,

dropping crumbs.

Cherry Pink

Seagulls graze on sky above the nursery,
clouds yawn and stretch apricot and violet
into powder blue and china white. Night

is late. In the playground a swing sits still,
overlooked by a squad of toys that squat
on the sill poking fun at the empty yard.

Cherry pink chalk matchstick men march
across tarmac, the wooden horse needs
a child on its back, a lick of paint. Night

is late. It's the anniversary of Mr Perry's
death. They found him a year ago today
swinging like lead from his garage roof

in a zero of rope. The news was translated
for the kids by parents reduced to innocence
and a rash of gossip spread across the tabloids

before anyone said a word. I remembered
the date on the bus, got off at the wrong stop
to come and feed the birds.

Happy Ending

He hooks stinking bait
on the dim pier, remembers
being a scuffed young lad
watching his father's hands –

massive plates of bone
and flesh stitching nets,
teaching him to thread
a needle in twilight,

how to balance on deck
when the sea was hunting
men and the rain failing
to escape desperate winds.

He owes it all to him…
where to find luck, a laugh,
how to pack a pipe and trust
himself to trust an anchor.

Last Wish

Everything beyond that door
is tidy as polished cutlery,

I unfold the perfect square
of starched cotton he gave me,

such unpredictable beauty.
A pill nestles in the tiny dimple

I smile at the notion
of a misunderstood kiss

and walk toward the window,
gatecrash the too familiar view.

Next door a black and white song
jumps, I think of the First World War,

pretty saucers, a flush of flesh
roses waltzing on bone china,

Madeira, liver spots and lavender.
The song jumps again and,

outside, a heartless car horn
warns a pigeon. A blue Citroën.

Behind me the mute TV throws
an advert for L'Oreal lipstick

into the mirror opposite. I swallow,
make an unexpected wish.

Black

Fumbling for keys in a black patent bag-

the only one I have with matching heels.
I bought them in the sales, a size too small,
a little too high, half price.

I find a damp handkerchief, a cough drop,
a broken string of plastic pearls,
a scrunch of bus tickets, my new red purse.

The host of sympathy cards and tags
that I picked from the bouquets and wreaths
now left to death at the head of your grave.

But you are in my safe-keeping drawer –
in a heat-sealed transparent forensic bag.
Your body is in God's custody, but to me

you are the pewter kidney-shaped lighter
that I had engraved for you with love
to wrap in the palm of your hand.

The stainless steel comb,
bay rum and dandruff
stuck between its teeth –

reminds me of the bald patch
our son Kevin has inherited
with your lisp and awkward jaw.

Your tobacco stained dentures,
an incisor chipped on a humbug
on a day trip to Clacton,

your stopped watch, wedding band
and the St Christopher that you drove
into black ice.

New Wound

That day caressed my head
anti-clockwise for the second time
in my small life.

The day that mum tried,
tongue-tied by heaven
to explain what a widow was.

I was just a mess of freckles,
scuffed white cotton socks.
Afraid to stand too close.

Terminal

I handed myself over like house keys
to a neighbour, and left destiny hooked on
a seizure like a shark locked in fresh air.
I was oblivious, nowhere to be seen
in that pale room losing weeks over sleep
between meals, milky tea and fussing shifts –

who changed their uniforms every day,
but wore the same perfume every day
so I always knew when it was Friday,
fish, chips and peas. My name was on the list,
filed under Terminal, my head a flood
of lost dolphins, drowning, trapped in the wreck.

Mavis

I met Mavis at a poetry group
that drank tea in a room of clumsy books
every second Tuesday of the month.

She predicted that I would be murdered
and clucked occasional clever questions
just enough to make me want to think twice.

She gave me weird advice, often sudden
like freak accidents, unexpected rain
but I always listened, just enough.

She was a deaf wasp, often slightly lost
in quick conversation and sloppy jokes,
kept a nappy pin beside the bread bin

'just in case' she'd say, I forgot to ask.

She had a crude grace, always told me off
for biting my lip, wearing red, drinking gin.
gave me all her unfranked stamps, homemade jam

and a purple crocheted mohair beret –
a kooky gift now snuggled in a draw
of other things that I will never wear.

She told me over tea and custard creams
when she had three to six months left to live
and showed me the watercolour again –

a bowling green, a sun-stained afternoon
painted by someone I'd met in her eyes –
a man who spoke in hesitant colours.

On March 1st she switched off like a light bulb –
no blood, no fuss, no time waiting for clocks
to stop. Nice, tidy, like her poetry,

edited once.

Claudette

I met Claudette at a poetry group
of lilac shampoo and sets, dress rings
Lavender and Blue Grass eau de toilette.

In spite of the years that lived between us
our clashing accents and bank balances,
we fit. Claudette, was a random blessing.

Her sling-backed fascination was reckless:
'So, tell me darling, what's he like in bed?
Has he got a good job darling, big house?
For Christ's sake darling please, at least a wife?'

She quizzed me into giggling and snorts,
coaxed me, teased me into seamless blushes
while we feasted on smoked salmon paté
and sherry, playing backgammon and chess

(decadent damsels in her attic-flat).
She licked her lips whenever I fed her
my second hand kisses like bulging grapes,
and I savoured her wise quirky advice,
her recollected life, romance, heartache,
the lovers, the deaths, the wars, poetry.

I need to think our schoolgirl banter helped
to bevel the cancer that nibbled her spine
like a conscientious rat. Her dark ache.

Toward the end I bought her acid drops,
slices of ripe pineapple wrapped in foil
to try and stave the blunt drug that suckled
the spit and merciless humour from her

I could see when she was ready to leave,
she simply stopped wearing lipstick one day.
The tears budded when I kissed her goodbye
in the hospice and bloomed behind my eyes
like impatient lemons waiting to burst
as the bus passed her flat on my way home.

Still Life

Since I stopped juggling water
it's easier to swallow spit,
chastise my appetite with a cigarette.

Anna tells me I am provocative
as a broken jaw when I sit monk-still,
naked and feral in her shivering studio

where a Russian radio faces the wall,
dirty-water-jam-jars mutter and the tap
drips into unwashed mugs and spoons.

I am stunned by her careless beauty
in this mess of gossiping curios,
immaculate details, broken things

where canvases hang, sit and stand
at indifferent angles. Anna's breath
is an Aspirin plume in this bitter place.

She reinvents me every week-
oil, pastel, charcoal, ink,
each stroke surgeon-soft,

she tells me to stop looking
for the moon in my handbag
and we laugh just enough.

But I can still smell blue cheese-
aggravating the fridge that night
he unpacked his temper and left

the future   ajar
no matter how carefully
she paints over the cracks.

Weird Fear

I sometimes miss the weird fear
I used to feel here years ago

on this landing, nineteen floors
closer to the clouds, nineteen floors further

from the bus home, a cup of tea, a hug.
I used to bite my lip and fidget here

where boarded up smashed-out windows
queue in rows like neglected teeth

I didn't understand then- the letterboxes
fenced with chicken wire and mesh

the keyholes shut up with crusted glue
or gagged by clumsy-cut plastic and wood

drilled in by bigoted nails.
I sometimes miss the kindness

of ignorance that age and experience
have helped themselves to.

Italy

On the balcony under sallow light
I hear a vicious scream to the left
of outside, imagine high heels, a broken

smile, an end. Italy has changed too much
or perhaps I haven't changed enough?
I remember the intermittent summers

spent here scavenging for a head start,
an emergency exit out of the everydays
stacked into a slow lifetime in Brighton.

But now the aisle, the mosaic tiles
of St Martin walking toward the altar
hand-in-hand with a crippled child

hardly matter.

Dislocated

She abandoned her desk
to walk in the park
watch the life she dislocated

when the past was on her side,
before she sold her ticket home
to buy crusts for the birds.

She likes this naive season best
before the snowdrops melt,
tulips hang their heads in shame

and the dairy cool breeze
chases its tail through the trees,
stirring great globes of leaves

like schools of nervous fish.
The months before summer
turns, cunning as tobacco.

She waited, unplugged and thin
in a room with a starched view
for him to return her calls but

he mislaid a promise to visit
somewhere between the lines
in a letter she still reads aloud.

Drifter

He sits with November,
his broad shoulders
chiselled into the sky
by tired light,

a restless fisherman
on the brink of an ocean
that has cast him aside
like a thirsty fish.

Soft Inch

I didn't *get* Jimi Hendrix
until you held my left breast
in your absolute hand,

pressed yourself against
my fit and I became
gracious albeit

for the lack of
a simple thing,
patience.

I am inclined
toward burst toys –
a pulse grinning

under a cuff,
that small warmth
under a watch strap –

the soft inch
made for a bracelet,
a button or a blade –

Unfinished Business

We know you are doing it on purpose
smuggling that polished penny
into my glass case

*you will always leave me
I will always insist you do*

because we are hapless romantics
in spite of ourselves. You set traps
and thrill me with deliberate tricks...

*the future is just butter in our mouths
the past...smoke between our toes*

you plant fun in my life (like the rose
you conjured from punctuation marks
and texted me unexpected as).

*we reminisce about 2 Tone and youth club
kisses on doorsteps kisses at bus stops.*

You know your grin still undresses my smile
and how I relish pretending to be helpless
rapt and bewildered under your spell –

*but now we have lived the lyrics sung
by Lloyd Cole and Everything but the Girl*

– I will never admit that a part of me is
because we can't afford to interrogate
the uncertain temper of risk.

*The raffle of receptionists know we are
another couple thirty years too late*

so let's lie warm, tell the truth until dawn
kiss if and when it is mutually convenient
in this web of rented beds we've spun

*because we invented kisses on doorsteps,
kisses at bus stops.*

Surrender

The sky is a menace of vultures
circling like paranoia overhead,

autumn's starving oaks and cedars
buckle like my mother's knuckles –

branches sketch charcoal profiles
across deaf clouds that swell rain.

I sense her at my shoulder again,
humming broken songs…

the widow, draping profound shadows
as November makes its last request.

The opaque moon proffers a shy light
seducing the view like a grinning tumour.

Summer, now sucked senseless
as auburn and amber leaves surrender,

and tall trees cower under threadbare
veils of frost.

Winter flexes its fist in the forest,
I shiver in thin wool.

Regret

I gave it freely
gift-wrapped in skin
so the smell of me
would hold his hand
when he drove home

alone

I watched
a clot of cloud lurk
around the moon
like a handsome gangster
a stray star lingered,

an afterthought.

Restless

A random starling
scribbles black
across the sunset,

a blade of moon
naps in the west,
a patient diamond.

You anticipate mist
as twilight hovers
nervous as a first kiss.

A complication of leaves
swan across the pond
before sudden rain.

Then a restless dog
barks in a distant yard,
reminds me of home –

the turquoise silk dress,
how its intimate stitches
still make me envious,

of the jigsaw pieces
dice and ribbons
that I've stolen for fun.

That I am and always will be
a jealous painter.
Frantic as blank canvas.

Moving On

Trinkets and gifts
from names I've forgotten,

a painting I've stopped
trying to understand,

books I still intend to read
and poetry that I can't.

The rocking chair that's fought
its way through two wars, three wills,

and the lemon paper swan
from a one night stand

that I still smile at on the bus.
A quick-sketch landscape

from a workshop last summer
where I tried to collect hobbies –

easy reasons for chit chat
at parties and things to do

with my hands to help me
stop smoking, again.

9 lifeless bin bags, 15 boxes
stacked like will power

in the spare room.
The hostages I've captured –

photographs, recipes, love letters,
and The Overdose

when I put him back on the shelf.
Diaries scribbled in different moods,

rooms, inks, reaching back into the years
before I nose-dive into the view.

Here's to
New Beginnings

Since moving to Brighton Bernadette Cremin has won increasing praise for the range and depth of her poetry. She has published three full collections: Perfect Mess (Biscuit 2006), Speechless (Waterloo 2007) and Miming Silence (Waterloo 2009). Her poem Nadia was Highly Commended in the 2009 Forward Poetry Prize. A 'new and selected' is due from Salmon in Spring 2013.

Bernadette's one woman show Altered Egos features six monologues and poetry from her collections. The 'scratch' performance of the show was runner up, 'best literary performance event' at Brighton Fringe 2010.

The poems in Loose Ends were specially written for the pamphlet and have not been published elsewhere.

"Theme," says Bernadette, "is a ticket to anywhere. I courted a mess of notions and this collection is the consequence. These poems are testament to my belief that there is no such place as The End. Life is, by its nature, unfinished business.

"The collection is dedicated to my Mum's Dad - my grandfather."

Acknowledgements
Thanks as ever to Jan Goodey for his editorial and moral support, to John Davies for inviting me to write this collection and to all at Pighog for making it happen.